A GREEK STORY ADAPTED BY
MERYL-LYNN PLUCK
ILLUSTRATED BY PAUL WISHNOWSKY

CHARACTERS

Narrator 2
Chief Gardener
Narrator 1
King Midas
Silenius
Dionysus (a god)

Narrator 1: Welcome to the world of ancient Greece.

Narrator 2: It's a world that includes part of what we now think of as Turkey.

Narrator 1: It's a world of myths and legends, and kings and gods.

Narrator 2: We are in a fabulously wealthy kingdom called Lydia.

Narrator 1: The idea of using coins for money has just been thought of...

Narrator 2: ...for the first time, anywhere in the world.

Narrator 1: **Bizarre** creatures roam this land.

Silenius: Bizarre? Are you talking about me? I'm not bizarre! At least, *I* don't think I am. I'm just a plain old satyr – half man and half beast.

Dionysus: Actually, you *are* quite bizarre, Silenius, but you're also quite **congenial** to have around. In fact, I rather enjoy your company. You're one of my favourite creatures. I'd be ever so upset to lose you.

Narrator 1: King Midas is the king of this fabulously wealthy kingdom.

Chief Gardener: Hello, Your Majesty.

King Midas: Hello, Chief Gardener. You're doing a great job with this garden. Just look at these roses.

Chief Gardener: You are truly a lucky man to have such a wonderful garden, Your Highness. Not to mention a loving wife and a delightful daughter.

King Midas: Yes, there is all that, Chief Gardener, but… still… well…

Narrator 1: There is always a "but" with King Midas.

Narrator 2: Yes, King Midas is a truly **privileged** man, but he never feels satisfied. Something is always missing.

Narrator 1: Indeed, King Midas is an extremely **discontented** man. He's also quite greedy.

King Midas: These roses are adorable, Chief Gardener, but how I wish they smelled and looked even better. Goodness me, what's this?

Narrator 2: King Midas is looking at a pair of legs sticking out from under a rose bush.

Narrator 1: And what strange legs they are. They've got hoofs instead of feet!

Chief Gardener: I do believe it's a satyr, Your Majesty. Oh yes, it's Silenius. His master is Dionysus.

King Midas: Come out this instant, Silenius. You are **trespassing** in my rose garden.

Silenius: Trespassing? We satyrs can't trespass! ***(to himself)*** At least, I don't think we can.

Chief Gardener: Well, you're here without **permission**, Silenius. I'm sure that even the god Dionysus would agree that what you're doing is trespassing.

Silenius: Oh, kind sir… and Your Majesty… please don't tell my master, Dionysus. I was running an errand for him and I'm afraid I lost my way. I just sat down in this garden for a minute and I must have fallen asleep.

Chief Gardener: Your Majesty, I recommend we send word about this to Dionysus at once.

Silenius: I **implore** you not to do that, kind sirs. Dionysus is a wonderful master, but he is very quick tempered. He will be very angry with me. Goodness knows what he might do. He's capable of doing anything! Suppose I make a bargain with you? If you'll overlook my foolishness, I'll entertain Your Majesty with some amazing tales.

Chief Gardener: Your Highness, I *strongly* recommend…

King Midas: Actually, my life is a bit on the dull side just at the moment. I could do with some entertainment.

Narrator 2: So Silenius stays at the palace, delighting the king and his family with wonderful accounts of his adventures.

Narrator 1: After a week, King Midas takes the satyr, Silenius, back to the god, Dionysus.

Dionysus: Thank you for returning Silenius, King Midas. Despite his many faults, I'm very pleased to have him back all safe and sound. As a token of my **gratitude**, I would like to offer you any gift you care to name. I know you are a man of great wealth and good fortune but, if there is something you should wish for…

King Midas: As you say, I am indeed very fortunate. Nonetheless, there are one or two things I still desire. Hmm, let's see. Aha – I have it! I wish I had the power to turn whatever I touch into gold.

Dionysus: Are you sure about this, King Midas? Have you thought this through? Do you really need that much gold? After all, *everything* you touch is an awful lot of gold!

King Midas: I'm absolutely sure, Dionysus. Thank you for offering me anything. Turning whatever I touch into gold is definitely what I want.

Dionysus: Well, if you're absolutely sure... then I grant your wish.

Narrator 2: King Midas's wish is granted. He's **jubilant**. He's thrilled.

Dionysus: Thank you again, King Midas. I wish you every happiness with your new gift. But you will be careful with it, won't you?

Narrator 1: Straightaway, before the god can disappear, King Midas starts to experiment with his new gift.

Chief Gardener: Your Majesty, what's happening? The roses...

King Midas: Isn't this fantastic? Gold roses. Before long, I shall be the wealthiest and most powerful king in all of Lydia. I shall be known as "the king with the golden touch"!

Chief Gardener: But Your Highness, the roses aren't just golden *coloured* anymore! Now they're made of gold and they've lost their glorious **fragrance**.

Silenius: Your rose garden has gone all still and lifeless, Your Majesty. It's not really a garden anymore. It's more like a… well, it's become a statue.

Narrator 2: King Midas's garden *has* become a statue, but he doesn't care! He likes having a golden garden and what's more, it's now worth a fortune!

Narrator 1: He calls for food and wine to celebrate.

Dionysus: You're not thinking straight, King Midas. If everything you touch turns to gold...

Silenius: You won't be able to eat or drink.

Dionysus: Look, King Midas, here comes your daughter. Remember what I said. Just be careful that you don't...

Narrator 2: But, before King Midas can stop her, his beloved daughter rushes into his arms...

Narrator 1: ...and turns to gold.

King Midas: Oh no! What have I done? I must get rid of this terrible gift!

Silenius: Only Dionysus can do that, Your Highness.

King Midas: Oh, Dionysus. Please forgive a stupid, greedy man. What must I do to get my daughter back?

Dionysus: It's most unusual for me to take back a gift, King Midas. That's not how it works. But, if you are *truly* **repentant**...

King Midas: I am, I am, Dionysus! I truly regret being so greedy. I'll do anything you say.

Dionysus: Very well. If you bathe in the river Pactolus the gift will be undone.

Narrator 2:	And that's precisely what King Midas does. As he steps into the river Pactolus, the sand beneath his feet turns to gold, of course.
Narrator 1:	But at that very instant, the power to turn things to gold leaves King Midas.
Silenius:	King Midas returns home a wiser man.
Dionysus:	He is greeted by his beloved daughter…
Chief Gardener:	…and a garden of colourful, fragrant roses…
Dionysus:	…having found true contentment.